30 YEARS TO DUBLIN

AN IMMIGRANT'S STORY

DÁRÁ NOLAN

30 years to Dublin
Copyright © 2020 by DÁrÁ Nolan

Tellwell Talent
www.tellwell.ca

ISBN
978-0-2288-2268-4 (Paperback)

Table of Contents

INTRODUCTION

I left Ireland when I was seventeen, just in time to walk into one of the worst financial recessions to hit Canada in decades. I bounced around doing any work I could to make a living and to catch the Canadian dream.

In my forties I had the pleasure to work with a Jewish Plumber named Richard Bieler who wrote poetry. He would walk into our Carpentry Shop proudly reading his poems to anyone at work who would listen, about all subjects including visits to the Foot Doctor entitled "My Left Foot" etc. I used to joke that he was our in-house Leonard Cohen. He was actually born in China while his parents were fleeing Nazi persecution in Europe just before the Second World War. He had spent time in Brazil before settling in Canada to raise a family. He wrote poems about his life experiences.

Unfortunately, Richard was killed by a car while out jogging one morning. It was a shock to everyone. I decided to write a poem in his honour. It wasn't very good, but it conveyed our shock and loss and was put into our work newsletter. I had the pleasure to meet his wife and adult children at a plaque dedication for him. They were pleased I had chosen to honour Richard with a poem and said I needed to continue writing poems as it would be a continuation of his legacy.

I didn't really think I ever would. However, over time, I began writing poems on my reflections of the way I grew up in Ireland in the seventies and eighties and my experiences as an immigrant in North America.

This is an accumulation of 7 years of reflection, regret, nostalgia, and gratitude. Without my wife Suzanne's encouragement these poems would still be in my bedside table waiting to be read by my children after I'm gone.

Without Richard's inspiration I never would have put pen to paper. I nearly called this book "The Jewish Plumber and other stories."

Without the people mentioned in these poems, by name or otherwise, I wouldn't have had the experiences (for better or worse) reflected on here.

So thanks one and all for reading them. I hope you find some of them relatable. I think they speak to what we refer to as the "Irish condition".

CRUMLIN

Nostalgic ghosts come back to dance in the sunshine.
We try to recapture an emotion that has flown,
along with the youth that housed,
but could barely contain it
A pang of longing that is hard to define.
Possibly reincarnation making itself
known for the first time.

Distance so immense separating
the adult from the child.
The other children only exist now
in middle-aged memories.
A yearning for a hometown is now
replaced with a yearning
for a childhood free and wild.

Recalling warm summer evenings
surveying the world from atop the stone tower,
Exploring summer meadows and hills that fell victim
to greed masked as progress,
hiding in tall cemetery grasses,

held there by its timeless power,
and remembrance of trudging through rural villages
on rainy Sunday mornings,
huddling together on the bus ride home for warmth.
All gone so quickly and without warning.

Taking a stand for black and white beliefs
long faded to grey.
Trying to forget unyielding convictions
that have been rendered unimportant by time.

Heroes knocked down from their
high pedestals years ago
are now just human.
Just the memory now of being so strong
and in our prime.

PORTMARKNOCK

Diesel fumes
as the bus idles.
Mass is over.
The sun is still shining.
We are waiting
for bellies to calm down or be sick,
as we choke
on smoke from the upper deck.

Onto the cold sand we run,
broken glass glinting in the early light
like shark fins
breaking the surface of the sand:
proof of drunk sins
waiting to slice into soft flesh.

Children yell
"Pie! Pie! Come out!"
at upturned buckets of sand
as ocean swells
sweep them out to forever with the tide.

Feathers and razor clams adorn
cakes made of sand –
shells for sprinkles
seaweed for marzipan.

The promise of crisps and biscuits
if you're good,
Burnt crusts snatched
by swooping gulls.

Tea and sandwiches
on tartan blankets,
ice cream moustaches
on babies in carriages

Discretionary towels
used to change into trunks.
Drooling dog jowls.
Chasing sticks into the surf.

Mothers call
"Don't swim out too far!"
The crab crawls
to its place among the evening stars

Folded prams
lifted back onto the bus.
Little hands
jars of Pinkeens tightly clutched

Fresh sea air exhausts any fight
from little heads touching pillows.
Day gives way to night
and is committed to memory

PEARSE PARK

Used syringes and condoms lie as
testament to last night's binge.
Brown and green glass shards create a puzzle
spelling out desperation as youthful dreams unhinge,
lads getting braver with every flagon that they guzzle.

The bloody stab wounds contrast with
the green shirt they stain.
Glue sniffers, with bag to mouth, watch indifferently.
The bystanders not getting involved,
resume their queen's games,
but, the action of the few has changed
the day of the many significantly.

Stolen sunburns acquired between intermittent showers.
The lexicon of love is heard all across the summer.
The bored kids destroy the freshly blooming flowers.
The engine revs and squeal of tires send
the children running for cover.

My senses are filled by the smell of
asphalt after freshly fallen rain.
The serene evening is broken by
the wino's off key refrain.
When the car alarm goes off they
know exactly who to blame.
Going home to bed past piss, graffiti and
desperation down Pearse Park Lane.

A place where it's claimed that they eat their young.
Victims of circumstance, opportunity
never shining on their face,
where too many verses of "The Ould
Triangle" have been sung.
Indifference and bad luck has kept
them manacled to this place.

Burning bonfires and wild children with
no parents to make them behave.
The guards try to contain the
mayhem, knowing it's in vain.
The natives always lashing back from cradle to grave.
Only fools go after dark up Pearse Park Lane.

A MOTHER'S LOSS

I've met you many times,
your face an obscure blur within my dreams.
Subconsciously we have embraced and bonded,
or so it seems.
We've only met each other for a moment
in time.That was oh so brief,
yet departing fills me with great loss
and the deepest of grief.

How can a blessing bestowed be a
hurdle to life or career plans?
Because they've never lived it, they'll never understand.
I try to not be angry at those who
look a gift horse in the mouth,
and at first hint of abnormality, choose to opt out.

Setting eyes upon you has confirmed the
instinctual bond I knew we always had.
I know it to be eternal now and, for this my heart,
though breaking, is truly glad.

Some higher power has decided that
this is how it must be.
I've been touched by your light and soul and
will carry it always with me.

I have to let you go for a while my precious child
down a different branch on this river.
Someday the waters will merge again
and we'll be reunited forever.

FIRST CHRISTMAS

Winter came overnight that first October.
I almost lost my life following fashion.
Waiting for the bus, my frost bitten
ears made a good distraction.
Until New Year's, I worked hard not to be sober.

That was the first time I ever had cash or a wallet.
Oh! The Christmas lights with their picturesque glow
an American TV dreamscape of drifting snow.
Leaving the bars, I felt a homesickness
I refused to acknowledge.

Back home they would be already
back from midnight mass.
Light would be creeping into morning over the frost.
They would get to see family later
and perhaps share a toast.
"What's the weather like there?"
Through expensive phone calls
friends and relatives would ask.

A billion snowflakes piled up outside,
one for every mile I was away from home.
I could only presume that it would soon get better,
I could never go back a failure, too much pride.

My Da went off to his new Canadian
bed dazed that Christmas eve,
turning off the light. The garage sale
décor faded into the background
and the gas furnace in the basement
made the only noise.
I sat in the dark watching music
videos of snow, and I cried.

WORKING ON THE LINE

Working on the line.
See the monkey doing his unskilled labour,
trading in his health for wealth,
trying to keep up with his neighbour.

Working on the line.
Repetitive motion injury strain.
Doing Jumbles, crosswords or Sudoku's
to force stimuli into the brain.
Listening to upbeat music designed to kill the blues.

Working on the line,
turning down the overtime.
I could use it to buy more stuff,
but my brain is numb and my body's had enough.

Working on the line,
drama unfolds when they go open secret stashes.
Alco's buzzes begin to take hold.
Take your pick Oxycodone, booze or hashish?

Working on the line,
rivet heads coked out, dancing at two in the morning.
A pill popper lies passed out on the floor.
Domestic disputes go off without warning.
The popper is back after six weeks
of rehab to pop some more.

Working on the line,
you wish you could just quit and walk away.

Where else would you get this kinda pay?

You heckle supervisors to pretend you have control,
and for a split second it doesn't own your soul.

Working on the line
Doing everyday what I've come to resent,
watching as my soul slowly gets destroyed.
Tears of desperation running down my cheeks
as it claimed the best years of my life.

Working on the line,
my loved ones all asleep in their bed,
I think about our fights, replay them in slo mo.
I'm here; the assembly line must constantly be fed;
my mind drifts darkly to where it shouldn't go.

Working on the line,
ten and a half hours on days or afternoons.
I drive home under ghostly moons,
spectres in the graveyard shrouded in mist,
wondering, is there more to life than this?

Working on the line.
Money is the drug, a short-term motivator.
This place plays tricks on your mind.
I came to realise much later,
To the damage it does. I'd been wilfully blind.

Working on the line,
the shackles are now broken.
For my freedom, believe me, I have paid.
Physically my body is healing but
the mental scars are slower to fade.

SINNER'S SOUL

Ma, tonight please offer up your
prayers for my sinner's soul.
Use your faith and influence! Tell them I'll atone!
Call in a favour and get me back into the fold.
Let them know I'm sorry and that I
didn't mean to be so bold.

Have all the armies of angels and
saints standing by your side.
Convince them that there's hope yet
beyond my pig-headed pride.
Convey to them my intentions.
Ultimately I only meant well.
I'll continue on mindful that good
intentions pave the road to hell.

So please pray to Saint Jude to bring
me back from around the bend.
Ask Padre Pio to join his hands back together
again, once they start to mend.
I ask you to convince the Saints, many
of whom you call friend,
to keep me in their prayers tonight, lest
I should meet some unholy end.

BONKOL

Morning milk rounds,
frosty bottles glowing in crates,
concrete bollards
try to deter you from this path.

Eyes adjusting to the light
in the factory down the alley
reveal a thick dusting of
neglect and hoarding.

Cardboard on wire screens
keeps out most of the rain,
an aged Golem unseen
In shadows behind the door.

Florence Nightingale is exiled.
Your injuries concealed like dark secrets.
Man or child, it matters not,
both live with regret,

The blackness of suicide
looms over unhallowed ground.
There's a warmth of sunshine
In walking away, and never looking back.

POLAR VORTEX

Winter has been so brutal
in its unyielding assault.
We choose to live here at its mercy,
so it's no one else's fault.

Clouds hang heavy and low
lumbering across the winter sky,
pregnant with the next birthing of snow.
The soul stifles an instinctual cry.

This season callously claims its victims,
both young and old.
However in spring time their voices are but a memory,
just like the icy sting of the cold.

For survivors, sleep brings no calm.
There is no physical or mental mobility.
Indifferent at best, seeming never to cease.
Bravely fought head on, but always in futility.

The twinkling darkness stretches
on, seaming to have no end.

Hints of warmth only come in small traces.
We pray for deliverance on cold dreary nights.
And by day wait hopeful for the sun to warm our faces.

GAME OVER

Walking away and down the road
we two are said and done,
neither ready to give the upper hand
to the other one.

It's time to go alone
down a chosen path.
We're no longer willing to suffer
each other's scorn and wrath.

The time has come to realize
this bough no longer bends.
Someday perhaps, in time
we can co-exist as friends.

Our deep infatuation
made us overlook incompatibility.
Once the passions cooled
we were faced with reality

Marry in haste and repent at leisure.
The little flaws, growing into crimes against humanity,
the discourse piling up in no small measure.
The arguments and petty wars pushed us to insanity.
We never said sorry,
when it was all that was left unsaid,
sleeping back to back
In a cold passionless bed.

Empathy should have been
something we could both feel
But, winning and control
were all we wanted from the deal.

Now we've parted ways,
and sleep in beds of our own making,
far removed
from the love we've spitefully forsaken.

HOLY JOE

Perhaps he fully understood the power that he had
to mould minds and shape futures,
giving inspiration to bravely move forward.
Holy Joe's classroom, it was my refuge.

While sheep conformed and dressed in grey
he wore cravats and flamingo pink coats.
Pulled on dapper jumpers over his head
without a hair tossed or pushed astray.

The Bleeding Stone of Knockacullen
still influences me to this day–
Getting high on life! A concept foreign
to the children of peasants.
He criticized the stink of stabbed-out
smokes when we came back to class,
And many inspirational words were spoken to save me.

Where many were intimidated by brutes in metal shop,
Some were screamed at for having no artistic skill.
Others were pummelled for their
ignorance in the octagon.
His was a kinder path of intellect and reason.

While he could see a country failing its youth,
and a kid foolishly giving up on his education,
his reference letter speaking of initiative and zeal
was a generous attempt to arm and protect
against an indifferent world.

JACKIE & MIRRELLE

Their names are seldom spoken in conversation,
but every morning they are invoked in silent prayer.
Their young lives snuffed out
and the abrupt end of childhood for others.

Out of body experiences watched from above,
Seen at a distance, bad news delivered.
Ma trying to break it gently.
"Both killed in a car crash," she said.
Me asking, "But are they okay?"

I was followed down to the river
just to make sure I was okay.
They needn't have worried
I was too stunned.
I couldn't even produce tears
for the river to carry away.

The headlines read in morbid black,
"2 dead in holiday weekend crash"

but I could picture the fieldstone wall
with brambles draped over the top,
first light revealing the little red car mangled into it.
I usually rode around in that car in their company.
However, fate had me in Canada this time,
lakeside beach tilt-a-whirl lights surrounding me,
instead of scars on a wall that had
stood since before the famine.

"We promise we'll keep in touch."
Promises that always fade with time.
Life intrudes on the novelty
and fifty promised letters become maybe five.

Her letter arrived a week after she died,
full of teen gossip and how I was missed,
plans to go away for the long weekend –
full of excitement and matter of fact.

She reminisced about us singing together
while we sat in the fields.
She wrote about fun, stupid things you do as a teen,
how a certain song reminded her of me.
Did she ever dream of her impending death at sixteen?

I understood, as a concept, the term heartbreak.
That letter's aspirations and optimism
made multiple stab wounds through
my heart, already homesick.
Yes, of that term I now had intimate knowledge.
I returned the letter to her Ma
along with a lengthy explanation.
It wasn't to upset her or prolong her grief.
I was just a friend sharing some of the
pain they were now facing.

Her older sister, who I'd once kissed,
wrote me back after a while.
My letter cheered her Ma up she said.
It had made them all smile.

Two years on, I searched for her grave marker.
I came to learn that it remained unknown.
She was interned with her Granda.
Too distraught, they hadn't put her
name on the headstone.

Jesus! Who could blame them?
The Garda delivering the news had the
door slammed in his face angrily.
She had told them she was babysitting with a friend.
It took time for disbelief to turn into agonizing reality.

I never heard anything more about Jackie.
There was a scene at his funeral.
His Ma attacked a taxi driver.
I guess people cope with grief in different ways.

Here we are 28 years further down the line.
In a photo Jackie and I wearing identical grins.
Damien still can't be a passenger on a car ride.
The broken jaw healed but the accident still haunts him.

Glimpses of memories clear and faded come to me
There's no lesson here, no redemption.
After the destruction of the illusion
of youthful invincibility,
there's only silence left, that of lost potential.

THAT DAMN COUNTRY SONG

I woke up this morning from a dream you hadn't gone.
I set a table for two; I understand now that it was wrong.
I grasped at the illusion and my mind just played along.
You see, I woke this morning from
a dream you hadn't gone.

I woke up this morning from a dream you hadn't gone.
My world was still a happy place,
where for you I could be strong.
Just for a moment I felt I still belonged,
but, then I woke up this morning
from a dream you hadn't gone.

I woke up this morning from a dream you hadn't gone.
The birds outside my window, they
refused to play along,
and pulled me out of slumber with
their high summer song.
They woke me up this morning from
a dream you hadn't gone.

I woke up this morning from a dream you hadn't gone.
You told me you'd never go.
I wanted to believe it but deep down
I knew it to be wrong.
I know you're gone forever but, still, I carry on.

Now I pray each night for dreams,
in which I believe you haven't gone.

THE TROUBLES

Reports of sectarian violence heard
between forecasts of drizzle and radio commercials.
Children radicalized in secret training camps
going through military rehearsals.

Leaders' holds on power only maintained
by keeping the violent status quo.
Defence contractors and funeral directors
profiting from people's misery.

Flag draped caskets of martyrs or the innocent.
Long funeral processions used not
to pay respects to the dead,
but to justify failed causes,
atrocities committed by both sides against
the backdrop of picturesque beauty.

Only our rivers run free but,
with the blood of our children.
Innocence dies quickly
when guns point at children sitting passively.

Loved ones imprisoned for fighting for the cause,
the cause being any act of violence
used to attain perceived liberty.
One man's terrorist is another man's freedom fighter –
cold consolation for the families of the dead.

Politicians denying the oxymoronic
term of all out "civil war."
Common knowledge that there has been nothing civil
since the troubles began.

The TV images safely framed and far away
now bleed into my reality.
Teens tarred and feathered for disobedience,

young men serving life on the blanket or
starving themselves until their eyes
fall into their sockets,
followed soon by death.

The opposing chants of "Not an inch!" and
"A nation once again."
Both may get their wish but
future generations will lament the missed opportunity.
Two tribes who will have chosen
annihilation over compromise.

nIPPISSInG

In despair I see the closing of a chapter in time.
I am forever yours but
painfully I realise
that you are no longer mine.

Pointing the way far north on to your destiny
Inuksuk's stand like petrified warriors on ridges.
Hope that you'll return safe is all that's left for me
As I strain to see light given by burning bridges.

Rolling through Gravenhurst,
the sun setting in the autumn sky,
I respect the need that propels you now
and prepare to say goodbye.

As we pass by Gospel Mission
I wrestle to make peace with your decision.
Driving you there so you can leave me is my penance,
my act of contrition.

All the moments combined
come down to this point in time- right now
I feel the old ones looking down with knowing smiles,
comforting us somehow.

If Honey and Baby wished to speak,
now would be good.
But, they have chosen to be silent,
remaining now forever in childhood.

You're breaking this old heart
with your ancient soul.
Time may take away the sting but,
I'll never be fully whole.

And just like that, you're moving on.
Mistakes I've made, remain forever wrong.
You have achieved for yourself full autonomy.
Lie to myself though I might, still
you are gone from me.

BILL C-51

Someone is shouting in the desert for all to hear.
The puppet masters caught off
guard now react with fear.
Their agents dive deep and switch to silent running.
The propaganda machine gets the
telegraph wires humming.

The blood red sun drips down behind the horizon
while your cell phone records your
every thought and word
and barrels of ink are consumed in
the spreading of their poison.
Luddites sharpen their axes, no
longer seeming so absurd.

Ask not: What is my country doing for me?
Ask: What is Big Brother doing to me?
What sinister fate awaits my family,
hidden behind a veil of secrecy?

The tattoo on my wrist
serves as a reminder to persevere,
making the traps of trust and indifference
all too clear.

Branding people who see through them
as the tin foil helmet crowd.
Rumours of abuse and torture
are strenuously disavowed.

The whistle blowers brought to trial
are placed out on parade.
Revenge is thinly disguised as justice.
All a masquerade.

The masses feel the blood in their temples
thrumming but they are too far under TV's spell
to prevent the changes that are coming.

On your chest you wear the medals
of one who's seen too much.
On your soul you bare the branding
of one who hasn't done enough.

Well past midnight now
the blood runs slow in sleep.
Uneasy dreams come of rights you'll give away
but know that you should keep

Who will win an election campaign
based on the fears of the nation?
Yet again it will be apathy
winning by acclimation.

LANDED IGNORANT

Are you not the stranger who arrives
in search of fortune?
Do you not surrender all that you have known?
Will you not fall into the hands of the exploiters?
Without mercy, will they not leave you as skin and bone?

Futilely you will struggle to try and stake your claim.
Will you notice how quickly your accent fades away?
You will have sold your soul once you change your name
Will it be poverty or shame that compels you to stay?

Have you not left the safety of home
in pursuit of a dream?
Were promises of fortune to be made
nothing more than lies?
Will you have anything to show for
all your efforts and schemes?
Or are you destined to keep toiling under icy skies?

Dispatches still come to you from the old world,
mostly bad news of those who have finally passed.
When you sit content with your new life and family,
will it matter that the snow has covered
the pathway back home?

STIGMA

Missing, out there wandering in the haze
Oh brother, where art thou?
with the past behind, living in the now,
with this affliction on you down all the days.

Storm clouds threaten,
always looming on the skyline.
We wonder, is this the calm before the storm or,
will things soon brighten?

Still waters, they are known to run deep.
Big boys don't cry.
For so long, this millstone
you've had to carry and to keep.

All is calm now, the violent eruptions
ended when you were young.
When the wind is right,
whiffs of smoke reach our noses, smoldering.
There's a chance this volcano may not be done.

Wounds still angry and open
To endure all that you have seen
You have gazed upon its ancient face
Horror for which no words can be spoken.

A departing embrace telling more
than a million words could say
Pain communicated by some unspoken language
The knowledge it will be yours
To carry until your dying day.

Those who cause the stigma may be
converted on the road to Damascus
For now you'll keep it hidden
If we'd known, perhaps we could have helped
but you're too ashamed to even ask us.

TROUBLED SLEEP

So now only mad men are at the controls.
My off spring tease me with an undercurrent
of contempt in their words.
None of us like what the future appears to hold,
And now I watch my mother navigate
through fog spells of dementia.

I continue rolling along, reciting
my prayers for the dead,
the number growing with every advancing season.
In these troubled times you receive
visitors to the edge of your bed
and life reaffirms for me that there are no guarantees.

Everyday I'm very close to bringing ruin
and destruction to my door.
The rain and darkness pushing in
against my driver's side window.

15 weeks sober and the black dog still
in pursuit across the moor.
From optimism to despair, the
pendulum swings to and fro.

A maelstrom of ghosts and demons try pulling
me into the underworld screaming.
I wake with my feet tangled in the sheets.
The alarm clock's red glow tells me
3 more hours of unrest.
On the leaf strewn dark roads, it's
easy to question your beliefs.

THE DODDER

They don't know how close they came that Sunday
to losing their youngest boy.
The Dodder with its deceptively gentle flowing pace,
still enough to consume a child.

My cousins pulling shop dummies
in from the river with a fishing rod.
More than once
they realized too late they were
actually bodies of the dead.

The Dodder drifted by the Georgian
homes in Clonskeagh.
Cousins on adventures while the
grownups relaxed inside
with biscuits and strong black tea.

How we ran and jumped about on the slippery rocks
in our scuffed leather shoes
and Duffel coats with buttons of faux elephant tusk.

The first thing you feel falling in
is the coldness as a shock.
I stayed in there paralyzed with fear,
my heavy duffel absorbing water so quick.

My cousin Thomas was the one who
pulled me out onto the riverside.
The kids were all stunned into silence.
I sat there in the sun while my clothes dried.

"Don't tell any of the grownups or
we'll all be in trouble!"
Later when questioned about my damp shoelaces
I told them I had been splashing in puddles.

Hard to believe that was over forty years ago.
Thomas is gone now, my children are grown.
Idyllically, the Dodder, still it flows.

CANADA I FEAR YOU

Canada I fear you –
your vast woods to the north
where bears and wolves wait for my missteps,
your frozen lakes that stretch on to the horizon
luring me out with your beauty
only to break the ice and consume me.

Canada I fear you.
The drifting snow waits to cover my frostbitten limbs
where they'll be discovered in the spring thaw.
The raging rivers hope to tenderize my body
on the boulders downstream.

I fear your cities that drip with opportunity
for the old money who've always owned it.
After all, I was not born here and ignorance is weakness,
and weakness leads to death.
My children were born here and do not fear you.
They stand tall and embrace your higher education.

Canada I respect you, but I will always fear you.
I will remain here, but in the relative
safety of your cities.
My bleached bones will still emit this fear
when they are buried under your soil.

TWENTY-FIVE YEARS LATER

Optimistic
Crossing feather bed hills going west
Fatalistic
Returning in disillusion back east
Maternal bonds lost
Long weaned from her breast

Reflections
Of life in a hazy past
Suspicions
Long held emerging from the dark
Questions
Answered but still to no end

Resurrection of the dead
Wooden head shovel quietly slicing the clay
Fruition of a plan
Begun many years too late
Ripened curiosity
Finally being sated

Wine soothing the sting
Brittle peace is made
Grudges of youth
Are now put to bed
Cold rain falling
As dogs slumber on

The tower stands
Stoically reaching into the sky
As you ascend
Time now obscures the view
You can't even see
The forest for the trees

Generals laid to rest
Find no peace in sleep
Their legacy strewn in
Granite fragments across the grave
Mixed with frost
Sparking in the morning sun

Anger and tears buried
In a smooth worn urn of ashes
The fog of history
Wiped clean from rose-coloured glasses
Closure comes now
With the burden of acceptance

Youthful looks
Long gone
A stranger walks
Streets which time has narrowed
Familiar now
Only by the stitch of his Aran

THE BICYCLE THIEF

Ann cycles along with him sitting
on the carrier on the back,
a cushion there to stop complaints about
the metal cutting into his arse.
alternating his grip between the
saddle springs and her hips,
the same hips that bore him into this world.

Against wind and up hills
he feels the gentle side to side motion
as she pushes the pedals.
The Triumph 20 has only three gears
and she isn't afraid to put them all to use,
taking her youngest everywhere
through streets and past meadows.

Nanny Eileen takes her oldest grandson,
the apple of her eye, to a bike shop in Dolphins Barn.
In the red and gold glow of his shiny new Raleigh,
the other two are given 50p each to ease the sting.

To the village on Saturday mornings
to get messages on a ten speed that is taller than him,
the carriers loaded with two catering
pans, sausages, rashers and the like.
"Such a great little messenger." Except the
times when things get mashed or cracked
"Those eggs aren't free! Be more careful on that bike!"

Some gestures are never forgotten.
His brother buys him a BMX.
He gets two years of pure joy from it
before, even with its flat tire, it gets stolen.

He rides a 10 speed he gets for Christmas,
cycling to Greenhills to be educated everyday
up and down on roads that eventually lead to nowhere,
managing to navigate and survive the
Walkinstown Roundabout.
After four wasted years, why would he bother anymore?

Once he realizes dead end jobs are his only prospect,
he joins up with the bicycle thieves
to make some quick money.

Stealing from schools, hospitals and backyard sheds.
Any place opportunity knocks, they answer,
as long as what they're doing can be hid.

The money doesn't offset the shame he feels.
He knows well that feeling of loss.
If he sees someone he knows,
he keeps his face concealed.

The bicycle thieves travel through villages,
towns, forests and mountain tracks
taking or receiving charity along the way.
Scandinavian girls with bare breasts
cupped against the window panes
were another distraction from the missing
brakes on the steep descent back.

Long after the bars have closed, bus fare now spent,
when he's still in search of a free ride home or a lift,
while he's dancing in the moonlight,
Phil Lynott's ghost talks to him,
telling him it's time to rise above this.

He rides his bike now in the boreal forests,
his youngest in a chair attached to the back,
his oldest with her training wheels struggling to keep up.
He is ever watchful for bicycle thieves
standing in the shadows.

ICE STORM

The ice pellets sound like grains of rice against the glass.
The winds howl while they snap off tree
limbs, accountable to no one.
Your scorn now has me in its sights.
I feel your contempt emanating from the other room.

The foxes dance about in the darkness,
their black silhouettes are shadows against the snow.
In there, somewhere, is a little of
our spirit in their routine.
But I remind myself that, that was a long time ago.

The cabin fever is quite high but the
fire is now all but embers.
The wilting roses still hint at how dear to me you are.
Finches outside battle the wind to reach the feeders.
Blackness has consumed your mind and
I'm not the man I used to be.

Winter has decided to stake its claim
and spring has been usurped.
Good decisions and reason are no longer on the agenda.
Sawdust and horsehair burst from
the punching bag seams.
My body and mind are fatigued
from being the lynch pin.

Today will pass and for once I won't be the strong one.
The cards can fall where they may, for
the moment they'll stay unclaimed.
This ice storm will do damage and cull its victims.
Upon its passing, we'll pick up our first
world problems and carry on.

THE FUNERAL

Here we have funerals, here we have wakes.
Here God and Devil fight over
whose soul is theirs to take.

We're a superstitious lot who leave out
salt and water on all Hallows Eve.
We touch the dead to make sure they
don't come back in dreams.

We say, "They're probably looking down on us all."
We cry and paw over the shell in
the coffin down the hall.

There's no memorial services here with
the dead a distant memory.
Here we display the body in all its wasted glory.

No cremation performed to cover up the evidence,
just tears and sorrow as we sing in remembrance.

We pray, cry and toast, even though broken hearted.
We sit with them as they become the faithful departed.

Chanting the rosary to drown out the Banshees' keen.
We mourn but don't forget, celebrating
the life that has been.

JUDAS

It was no fallen angel
betraying you for 30 pieces of silver.
It was only a disciple
whose faith began to waiver.

With the giving of a kiss, a prophecy was fulfilled,
a role was played.
Blood of the innocent was spilled.
Both our fates were sealed.

You entered into your passion
just as the cock crowed.
To try gain absolution,
a hemp cord placed over a bough.

Sitting at the right hand of the throne,
commanding that we turn the other cheek,
oh preacher of forgiveness, will you
not bestow your mercy
on one who was only human, one who was only weak?

SMACK

A mighty storm comes from the east.
Sheets blow on clothes lines in the flats
like sails billowing on clipper ships.
But tides missed, anchors keeping them moored.

Conditions ensure a perfect storm,
stripping away the last of Hibernia's innocence,
taking more than eight hundred
years of empire ever could,
and leaving hopelessness in its wake.

The high! Oh the fucking high!
The pin prick dulling the glassy eyed pain.
The euphoria lasts not nearly long enough.
Reality and its cravings soon return.

Purchasing the lie of eastern promises,
wanting the "more" that can never be attained,
the callous profit from desperation,
building their palaces in fields of blood.

The plague runs through the streets
devouring and never being sated.
Skeletons lie strewn about the river banks and valleys.
The used dry up and blow away like leaves in the breeze,
all observed from the refuge of monastic towers.

Now we pass haunted places lit by the moon.
Ghostly silhouettes shrink back from the windows.
Skeletal faces recede into the darkness to die,
having the decency to do it out of view.

ANGRY HEART

Don't feel like you could have done more.
Don't think you could have stopped this
world from tearing me apart.
Things hurt less when you recognize and acknowledge
it's this world that's injected poison into my jaded heart.

Know you mean more to me than
any worldly possession
or accomplishments I've made over the years.
Understand I'm not built to look at the big picture,
that I was doomed to be devoured by my fears.

Take solace in knowing all of this was predestined.
We don't get to alter fates course.
Appreciate the time we get to steal for ourselves.
We'll always have that long after my
heart succumbs to its force.

Forgive my perceived anger
and the hurtful things I've said and done.
Taking a hardline wasn't a thing I could control.
The only victories I've known were hard won.

Fools have mistaken my kindness for weakness,
but I've never suffered bullies who
abused me whilst I toiled.
Experience has shown me that in the end
the squeaky wheel gets the oil.

Mislabel me if you must as born under an angry star,
but it's not in my DNA to walk away
turning the other cheek.
I'll keep fighting for what is right
until the earth is inherited by the meek.

ARMAGH ROAD

Sister Gemma scolds those who throw
stones into the puddles,
the concentric rings rippling out.
The black leather strap appears from under
her robe and is generously wielded about.
Sister Francis delivers the Catholic paper.
Her days of humiliating are long gone.
She is now afforded charity and kindness
by the very ones so wronged.

I hear them say, "But, we were happy
then. It was a much simpler time".
"We were happy then."
It's funny how nostalgia can cloud the mind.

The truant inspector pretends to take
away children who miss school,
through no fault of their own,
the same ones who carry head lice and are
only a covering of skin over bone.

Waxed parquet floors hold memories
of souls who trembled on them
in ignorance and fear.
The same ones who cleanse their thoughts today
with the antiseptic of drunken tears.

You can hear them say, "But we were happy
then, it was a much simpler time".
"We were happy then."
It's funny how nostalgia can reprogram the mind.

Mr. Lowe sells sweets off a bread
tray balanced on a pram,
and they are chewed in heads filled with cavities.
Kids' pants are torn on vandalized slides.
Mammys use safety pins to fix the pants
and save their baby's dignity.
I can't believe they say, "But, we were happy
then, it was a much simpler time."
"We were happy then."
It's sad how nostalgia tricks the mind.

The school is burning as a crying kid
is walked home by the arsonist.
His motives for both actions, to this
day, still remain a secret.

The children hurl rocks at bus
windows and away they run.
It only becomes a matter of time before they
graduate from the rock to the gun.

And they'll always say "But we were happy
then, it was a much simpler time."
"We were happy then."
It's tragic how nostalgia can warp the mind.

ANNIE'S SONG

When Annie's song on the radio came on
my heart lifted when you sang along.
To hear you sing is such a rare phenomenon,
your anxiety and disorders forgotten and gone.

My sunglasses hid the tears as they welled.
Such a bittersweet moment to keep in my memory:
I kept on driving, pretending to look at the road,
a moment more precious to recall,
I know there'll never be.

PADDY

I can't tell you I love you,
or express how grateful I am to you for
bringing me into this world.
It's something that's just not done.
I want you to know I'm eternally grateful
for your protection and guidance,
but still the words don't come.

Sometimes we talk on subjects as pretence,
to try bonding on common ground.
I'm sad because in the end we'll part ways
without ever acknowledging what
we both feel deep down.

There's a distance that doesn't get smaller.
As the years go by it remains vast.
Our emotions never seem to align.
Sometimes our souls are exposed
when we let our defences slip,
but our upbringing won't allow us to acknowledge it,
so we walk away for fear of a quivering lip.

No man is an island, but he's doomed to
remain isolated from his feelings
just like his Da, and his Da before.
We wait for deathbed confessions
whispered in a delirium.
This is the only time we dare venture remotely near.

I reflect on the man who carried me
through town to visit Hector Gray
after my shoes blistered my young feet.
Still I can't tell you my true feeling that I love you,
even though it's always close to the
surface, lurking just beneath.

THE BARONS OF CRUMLIN

The Barons of Crumlin sit atop the shop
canopy reviewing the parade
casting mocking judgments on the crowds below.

The verbal promises they make to each other
are only worth the paper they were never written on.
They tap ash from improvised smokes
that are only wooden toothpicks after all.

The steeple casts its evening shadow across the village,
the ocean beyond and the ages.

The dew sits atop the grass like pearls
waiting for the morning sunrise
to give them ascension to heaven.

The Barons wake on forested mountain side
with morning dew heavy on their robes
unaware this is their time in paradise,
that there is no further ascension,

that the empire of time will unseat them
and cast them into exile.

EILEEN

She told me
that for Christmas, you were lucky
to get an orange and a jotter.
She showed me
how they used a piece of bread as an eraser.
She warned me
about a ball-shaped thing found amongst the ashes,
another tall tale about a child who played with matches.

She limp-shuffled through the village
every Sunday up to Mass,
a figure slowly approaching in red
overcoat and matching headscarf.
"What is it ails ya?" she asked,
seeing the tears we all wept.
The fog of dementia couldn't block her pity,
as Da buried our dog Scotty by the fence.

She was superstitious about the colour
green coming into the house.
A green car almost killed her and
gave her a permanent limp.
Da would say she didn't mind green
when it was on Irish pounds.
Her old eyes strained through thick
glasses at newspaper print.

Every day, four sausages and peas
covered in candied sauce.
She liked to sit on the sofa, smoking a
Gold Flake as the world passed by.
To save on matches, she lit two cigarettes at once,
a cigarette in nicotine stained
fingers always held up high

They Irish say you should touch the dead
so you don't dream about them.
I touched her deeply etched face at
rest in the satin lined coffin.
The dark purple bruises peppered her
skin where the I.V. had been.
Not even the Rosary Beads binding her
hands could keep them hidden.

Twenty years later while sleeping, we felt her presence.
She looked into the crib at the newborn, her namesake.
She had come to see and give her blessing.
We woke to the familiar smell of smoke, her Gold Flake.

STARDUST

Forty-eight young spirits out for fun
on Saint Valentines Eve.
Forty-eight sets of hopes and dreams torn asunder.
No one in the city is untouched by the banshee's keen.
Forty-eight tombstones for future generations to ponder.

Saturday and the news washes over a
stunned nation intently listening.
Solemn visits begin to relatives across
the north and south of the city.
The hardest news is heard, Sandra is missing.
Brave faces conceal what they already
know in their hearts.

A statement that forever changes things.
Families pull together to hope against hope.
Soon enough word comes from Coroner's Court.
Cold clinical dental records confirm that all is lost.

The family gathers now to mourn
the loss of one of its own.
At the graveside Granda stands
watching his son bury his child,
He stands stoic, unable, though he
wants to, undo what is done.
The coastal winds blow, cutting at mourners
faces, unrepentant and wild.

This scene is played out another forty-seven times.
It need not have happened! I'll say
it, greed always succeeds.
They were trapped by an inferno behind chained doors.
Generations later and the innocent are still paying.

Monuments were erected to pay them tribute.
Politicians talk of inquiries, to this day.
On and on they drone,
but the fact remains, that they never came home.

Forty eight beds made up, Forty
eight beds still lie empty.

HER

She lives life on her terms, without an ounce of regret.
She won't admit she's sad, while
tears spill down her face.
She'll read your fortune in the cards,
but won't reveal their secret.
She keeps it well hidden, feels it's not her place.

She will always remember, but won't hold it against you.
She takes your transgressions and
leaves them at the river.
Despite your flaws, she still loves you.
After all, to your children, she is mother.

She laughs when squirrels steal seed left for the birds.
They have to eat too; she won't stop
them, just puts out more.
She has a vulnerability that you just can't put into words.
Yet, she is Mama Bear defending her
brood, to the last drop of blood.

She will act as your sober second thought,
but won't stop you from doing what you do.
She will guide and shepherd your conscience
before you can carry your foolish actions through.

She will tolerate the demons that torture her mind,
suffering in silence, while you're sleeping by her side.
She doesn't complain, just carries on,
saying everything is fine.
Claims she can't remember, when
you ask her about last night.

She'll endure pain that would make
Dogs of War scream.
She'll let you in after she has been into her cups.
She believes in angels, and tries to interpret your dreams.
Doesn't realize that she is one, on
you she never will give up.

DEFENCELESS CREATURES

So the kitten lay there with its throat
slit open and its head falling off.
Yet it continued to cry
and Mister McGinn told us he'd take care of it.
All the while he was the one who killed it,
but he stood there lying to the children's faces.

Standing in Carey's backyard with
paint on our clothes and skin
that turpentine and slaps couldn't remove,
Fray Bentos tins, the evidence of a bachelor's life
strewn about the overgrown backyard.

Fiona and Anita were showing me
their secret earthly treasures.
As I experienced what I remember as my first hard on
whilst Da observed from our scullery roof.

Ma pounced on me with Catholicism
exploding and oozing from every pore
"God will punish you for all your
sins! He sees everything!"
While all I remembered was how nice it
felt and the tightness in my trousers
when Anita undid her dungarees and showed
me what was hidden underneath.

I was probably seven at the time and never forgot.
It would be another three to four years before I
knew, let alone experienced, what an orgasm was.
Fucking Catholicism warping my
mind and filling me with guilt.
Priests filling our heads with fear:
"There are sins that God knows about and
he will cast you into eternal fire!"
Why don't you fuck off and worry
about your own souls!?
Fucking wolves in sheep's clothing

Don't check on the water temperature while
we're showering at the youth club,
saving the image for later to play
over in your deviant minds.
You gave me a playful spanking while
you draped me over your knees,
but I still remember the feel of your deviant
cock grinding against my belly.

Burn in hell for what you did to my
cousin, my poor defenceless blood.
He wouldn't comply with your perversity
so you turned his family against him.
If the punishment were to fit the crime,
you'd be laying there bleeding
with your throat slit, like a dying kitten.

SONNY

He walked down Walkinstown Avenue,
one shoulder sitting 3 inches lower than the other.
A life of carrying a bricklayer's hod
had made its permanent mark,
visible even when he wore his trillby hat
and coat over his slight frame.

He walked everywhere, to place a bet
or deliver a box of Milk Tray to each
of his six living daughters.

A man who as a child lost his father in the "Great" war,
who dug in the rubble of the G.P.O. for a fish knife relic
when it was left smouldering by the Brits.

A man who raised twelve of the
thirteen children he sired.
A man who watched his son bury his child.
A man who was nothing but class,
who would sit with quiet dignity smoking
a Christmas cigar in his armchair.

He walked to Dolly's grave at Mount Jerome.
Sometimes he met his children or grandchildren there.
The doctors sent Dolly home from the hospital,
on a mattress in a van to die.

It took six weeks of ranting and
raving in a bed in the parlour
before the cancer killed her.
Those old hearts were too strong to know when to quit.

All the kids knew that King Kong and Elvis were buried
Within the walls of this Victorian Cemetery.
The old gatekeeper who had become his
friend over the years asked us:
"Is it himself in the Hearse this time?"
We nodded a solemn yes.

The procession bell that signified a funeral cortege
tolled extra-long that day as he paid tribute to Sonny.

MA

During the Christmas season
Driving through snow covered Acton
past decorations warm and inviting,
the sky's blue reflected on ice.

Outside the church sits the hearse,
black and accusing in contrast to the snow.
On my lips the Christmas song
dries up and dies, like promises post-election.

I ask God in his heaven to forgive me.
Then, confident in my immortality,
my thoughts turn to you:
your death means the loss of the one
who brought me into being
and the confrontation of my biggest fears.

A million years from now, I hope I'll
honour my pall bearing duty.
I will carry a weight heavier than any grudge.
This yoke of your passing placed upon me
will be such a crushing burden.

A Brendan Behan image comes to mind so perfectly apt:
the child stands weeping at the grave.
He is fixated, he is rapt
as priests' prayers and rain pour down over us all.

The parting glass will be rinsed and left to drain
The silence will greet me when I call your number.

I'll take Comfort in the memory of your kindness.
Your selflessness will haunt me into slumber.

I'll stand at your grave while November
makes the trees groan,
and we'll talk as if you are still around.
But I'll know your soul has flown,
life's cruelty leaving me bereft.

GORTA

It was less than a year since John Lennon
had been silenced forever.
Bobby Sands had finally achieved martyrdom.
"The hunger strikers have vowed to
continue," said the old man next door.
The world was watching and the
Iron Lady refused to budge.
Ten of them would give their lives in the end.
My Da was worried it might start off a civil war.

My brother was being radicalized at work.
Compelling arguments were being
made by middle aged men.
My Da felt anger towards them for "corrupting
a young impressionable mind."

My cousin had just gone to prison for
making bombs for the IRA.
My Aunt could only watch in disbelief.
"He was just doing what he believed
was right!" said my brother.
"She's a widow and who'll look after
her now!?" my Da replied.

My Da had no love for either the
Crown or the men of violence.
He only had love for his son,
the one who didn't yet understand the consequences
of that dangerous kind of thinking.

My Da went to England as a newlywed in the 1960's.
On his first day at work all the men there
called them by his first name "Paddy"
The dark sarcasm was lost on this naïve immigrant.
Yes he knew discrimination, hatred and contempt,
but wasn't about to let it eat his firstborn.

He also had compassion for others
"What about people in England?" he would ask
"Blown up while doing their shopping or having a pint."
"Just working class people like us. It's not right!"

When political activists knocked looking
for support, he was never rude,
but when they left he'd shake his head.
Educated young men with such hatred
instilled in them by their fathers
who had been interned without trial.
Their crime was to be Catholic.

My Da had three sons to worry about.
He feared he could lose them to
radicalization or a sniper's bullet.
Canada with its bitter cold winters
looked more attractive everyday.

POETRY

There are those that say poetry is irrelevant,
that it simply doesn't matter.
They don't understand the compulsion
that forces you out of bed in the night
to nail your thoughts to paper before they fly away.

They may never have felt the push toward morning
as blackness recedes with the dawn.
They don't have to argue with the daemons
who've always been there living in the walls.

It's what separates us from the animals
and what keeps us alive when others act like them.
It has the power to make our words universal
and us immortal,
no matter how many hairpins are
driven through our tongues.

An idea can be viewed as a powerful thing
and poetry is an idea wrapped in passion.
Political prisoners the world over already know
it is the one thing that can't be
taken from their possession.

For poetry is an inuksuk that
directs us on through time,
showing us that others have walked this trail long before
and that though misunderstood, we are not alone.

ESSENCE

Throw my essence to the wind to scatter it far away.
Have it float on moonlight clouds
to meet the coming dawn
far East to Eire, where I spent my youngest days.

When it reaches that sacred place
where I commenced my life
have it visit silent Wicklow valleys
and blow around like Jinny Joe's caught up in the light.

Let it dance about like rabbits at the Curragh in the sun
Watch it settle as comfort on an old friend's hand
Showing them I'm still here, though
it seems that I'm gone

Let it subconsciously brighten their face
with the touching of their skin,
just like buttercups we placed as
children, underneath our chins.

Have it drift over fog-enveloped hills soothing
the cuts of my actions and my words.
Have it ripple gently by Grand Canal banks.
Let my conversation be heard in the singing of the birds.

Let it flow over Enniskerry waterfalls
kissing your eyes as mist.
May it fall like droplets of warm summer rain.
Let it remind you of when you were truly blessed.
Let it nestle on Hell Fire club roof tops,
where as kids we'd often go.
And when the night falls on that summer evening,
watch the twinkling stars blend
with the city lights below.

Make it sparkle like granite headstones
in Crumlin graveyard.
Make it glisten like rain under street
lights on dark Dublin roads.
See it converse with the ghosts who still ply
their trades unseen in the darkness.

Have it nourish the plants and trees,
returning to the soil at last,
where once again it takes its part in the cycle
Would that be too much for me to ask?